T0157520

I
HEAR
DESTINY
CALLING

TRINA W BATTLE

WESTBOW
PRESS®
A DIVISION OF THOMAS NELSON
& ZONDERVAN

WestBow Press books may be ordered through booksellers or by contacting:

WestBow Press
A Division of Thomas Nelson & Zondervan
1663 Liberty Drive
Bloomington, IN 47403
www.westbowpress.com
844-714-3454

Unless otherwise indicated, scripture quotations are taken from the Holy Bible,
New International Version®, NIV®. Copyright © 1973, 1978, 1984 by Biblica,
Inc.™ Used by permission of Zondervan. All rights reserved worldwide.

Scripture quotations marked KJV are taken from
the Holy Bible, King James Version.

ISBN: 979-8-3850-1142-1 (sc)
ISBN: 979-8-3850-1143-8 (e)

Library of Congress Control Number: 2023920843

Print information available on the last page.

WestBow Press rev. date: 11/09/2023

DEDICATION

"God is teaching us that thru adversity the character of God is worked. How else can longsuffering be worked except you suffer? We have entered into the fellowship of Christ sufferings. I have found that in my own personal experience when things are rough the glory of God rests upon you. Indeed, it is the suffering that puts on the shine. I just want to encourage you to go on in God. Be encouraged to press in to all that God has for you. You will never regret it.

-Gloria S. Harbison

In loving memory of Gloria Smith Harbison. We did it, Glo! We did it!

CONTENTS

INTRODUCTION

There it was in writing. Dated March 23, 2023, in my journal were the words "This year will be my last year at Mercury Industries (name changed to protect company's identity). Mercury Industries had been my employer for the last 9 years. I was twenty plus years in my career in Human Resources and this was the longest I had ever worked for an employer. I enjoyed working for this company. I felt heard and valued and I was earning more money than I had ever imagined. I remember saying to the Lord, "Lord, I want to earn enough money to pay all my bills and live comfortably. But I don't want to earn so much that I forget where my blessings come from." I wanted to earn a six-figure salary, but I didn't want a salary of that size to cause me to become arrogant or boastful. I'm grateful that He was kind enough to bless me with more than I requested of Him.

Not only had He blessed me in salary, but He also allowed me to drive every car I ever wanted and, we had just purchased our third home. It wasn't just any home. It was the type of home I had always dreamed of owning. Here I was in my 40's watching my childhood prayers being answered. While material things are nice, I had so much more. I had an amazing husband as well as beautiful children and grandchildren. God had blessed me with a man who not only loved me but desired to give me the world and more. Our children were thriving and though they were spoiled, they were good people with good manners. Life, by all accounts, was good. Really good.

In the moment I wrote that statement, not only were we a little over one year in our new home, but our last child was also on track to graduate from high school in a few months. Come August we would have two children in college and, my husband and I agreed that we were going to send them to college with no student loans. Yet here I was writing in my journal, "This year will be my last year at Mercury Industries." I was preparing to walk away from a job that no longer served me into an undefined, unidentified place. I literally had no idea what I going to do next. But everyday God was telling me it was time to leave.

Things at work had become so toxic and so bad that there were days I found myself crying in the car during my commute. Only to get there and hear my staff complain about how miserable they were and how they didn't want to be there either. But none of us could leave. Why? We were paid well. Where could we possibly go in the local area to earn the same or better salary than we were currently earning? It didn't matter that we were miserable being there; we had a job and financial security and to walk away from that would leave us and our families vulnerable and we weren't willing to do that. It seemed like a foolish idea. But God wouldn't let it be. He kept pressing me.

In the months following that journal entry I found myself going back to something I hadn't done in years. I began spending more time with God. You see, when I was single and living alone some twenty years ago, I spent most mornings in prayer and meditation. But after I became a wife and mom, my focus switched. When I was single and childless, I didn't have to make time for God. I had nothing but time and I enjoyed getting up and spending time with Him. He was everything to me and I longed to be in His presence.

But when I became a wife and mother, my focus became mom, wife and work and in that order. After I had completed all those duties for the day, I went to bed with a simple "Thank you, Jesus" and kept that same routine day in and day out. Yes, I would pray but I would only read my Bible occasionally and there definitely wasn't any time set aside for in-depth prayer and meditation. I recognized early on that my focus had changed and I was no longer serving like I should but I resigned myself to this new life and so I kept going in the same direction.

There would be times throughout the years when I felt guilty that I was no longer putting forth the effort to grow my relationship with God, but I would find a way to get pass those feelings; to somehow reconcile in my mind that all was well. God allowed me to get away with it for a very long time but now He was no longer putting up with me putting Him in last place. He was allowing a situation to occur in my life that was beckoning me back to Him. I had no other choice but to stop and listen.

Now every morning I found myself getting up no later than 5:45am. Normally I wouldn't even begin to stir until 6:15 or later but God was calling me to get up earlier. He wanted me to come meet Him. We needed to talk. He knew that if I waited until the end of my workday to spend time with Him, I would make excuses and not give Him my full attention. No, I had to get up early and I needed to be fully awake. So, I would get up, get dressed for work, make myself a cup of coffee and head upstairs to the Bonus Room to pray and meditate. Not only would I pray and meditate but I would also play music to calm my spirit before fully starting my day.

I've loved music for as long as I can remember. I could count on music to calm my spirit whenever I found myself moving into darkness. It makes sense to me why Saul would have David come play for him when his spirit was heavy. The right song is like water to dry, thirsty land. I didn't stop playing music when my quiet time was over. Many days I played the same songs on repeat on the way to work and kept them playing during my workday.

I was fighting a spiritual battle, and praise and worship were the bullets I used to fight the enemy. I had many favorites like Vanessa

Bell Armstrong's Peace Be Still and Kelonte Gavin's You Are My Joy. I would play Tasha Cobbs Leonard's The Moment and Lecresia Campbell's We Magnify Your Name. However, as I got closer to making a decision about my work situation, I had three songs on heavy rotation. Smokie Norful's I Still Have You, Micah Stampley's Another Place and Tye Tribbett's Only One Night. Each of them had significant meaning for my current situation.

When Smokie sang "I win even when the score says I lose" it was confirmation to me that walking away from a lucrative career didn't mean I lost. God was telling me that I was about to walk into something greater. There would be people who would wonder why and even how I could give up a job when the economy was in such bad shape, but I knew leaving would be winning. When Micah was asking the Lord to give us new levels and dimensions in Him, I knew that meant I would be moving closer to God and our relationship would deepen.

And every time Tye said, "only one night though", it was pure music to my ears. I have never been a person to dwell on any issue for an extended amount of time and he was reminding me that this time would be no different. Yeah, I could cry and be upset about my situation, but I had to keep it moving. We were never meant to dwell in misery. I always say, have your moment and then get yourself together. Ask God for wisdom and direction and get busy. Tye was reminding me that same sentiment applied to this time in my life.

I also found myself journaling more. God would often stop me in the middle of praying and tell me to write. He would have me write not only what I was feeling in those moments, but He would also bring certain scriptures to the front of my mind. The scriptures He would place on my heart were not scriptures that I would normally think about during a normal day, but they were familiar scriptures, and they were fitting.

No good thing does He withhold from those whose walk is blameless. (Psalm 84:11)

I was young and now I am old, yet I have never seen the righteous forsaken or their children begging bread. (Psalm 37:25)

Now unto Him that is able to do exceedingly abundantly above all that we ask or think, according to the power that worketh in us... (Ephesians 3:20 KJV)

For I know the plans I have for you," declares the Lord, "plans to prosper you and not to harm you, plans to give you hope and a future. (Jeremiah 29:11)

It's almost like He was preparing me for what was to come over the rest of the year. He wanted me to know that He had my back and that I had nothing to fear. Although the situation was weighing on me, I could feel Him working. He was pushing me to be obedient and He was pushing me to make a decision. Was I going to stay in the comfort of toxicity with a stable paycheck or was I going to be obedient and walk away? Decisions. Decisions. Decisions. To be truthful, even with all the encouragement these scriptures offered, I was still afraid. I had walked away from a job before with no plan and I vowed to never do it again. But this felt different. This felt right. Yes, somehow, I had to do this.

It is my firm belief that God placed people in my path to propel me into my destiny. Just so happens in this situation these people were my colleagues. They were people with an authority greater than mine and they controlled my destiny in the company. Their opinions carried great weight and if they criticized my performance, other people of authority, who knew little about me, would be compelled to believe them. While their deeds were self-serving, they had no idea they were being used by God to catapult me into a destiny that had already been written for me. Not even I at the time recognized what was going on but had they not lied to me for their own self-preservation, I would not have had a way to walk away.

The enemy meant to harm me by making me question my worth and my value. He didn't realize he was being used by God for a greater purpose. The people He put in my way to block me from promotion had no idea they were part of God's great plan either. Even to this day they have no idea how I have prayed for them from day one, asking God to meet their needs. While I didn't like what they had done and were doing, I did not want them to come to harm. I warned them that God didn't play about me but I still desired that they be blessed. Besides, whatever happened to them wasn't for me to decide. That's God domain and I trust Him to deal with them however He chooses. It wasn't long after everything had gone down that I realized they were placed in my life for a reason, and they had completed their assignment. God presented a way for me to walk away with provisions so that I could begin to walk the path He had created for me. And He used them to make it happen! *The steps of a good man are ordered by the Lord.* (Psalm 37:23 KJV) and I was about to take my first step.

I must be honest and say although everything was pointing me in the way of leaving, I was skeptical. Would I be able to find a job? Would I like this new job, or would I have to just take whatever I could find? Would the compensation be the same or better or would I have to take a pay cut? Surely God wouldn't have me walk away from a lucrative paycheck to get something less! Besides He had already told me the plan was for my bank account to overflow. He said that money would no longer be an issue for me and my husband and that my boys would be able to complete their undergrad debt free.

But I still struggled with saying yes until April 24, 2023, when He said to me, "I've already done it, Baby Girl. I'm waiting on you." Well Peter, I guess it's time for you to get out of the boat! And so that's what I did. And every now and then, just like Peter, I find my focus moving from watching Jesus to looking at my situation. When I take my eyes off Him, He politely nudges me and says, "Do you trust me?" and my answer has continuously been yes.

I had no idea that saying yes and being obedient to the voice of God would lead me on a journey full of ups and downs. For some reason I felt everything in my life would be smooth sailing simply because I let go of my will and fully embraced that of the Lord's. But it has not been smooth sailing. There have been moments of confusion and doubt. But those moments have caused me to have a better understanding of Romans 5:3-5(KJV),

> *And not only so, but we glory in tribulations also; knowing that tribulation worketh patience; and patience, experience; and experience, hope; and hope maketh not ashamed…*

Being obedient to His will has driven me to a deeper, more intimate relationship with Him. As much as I have known and loved God, I have never known and loved Him as much as I do now. In this season I am learning who He really is for myself and not just what I've heard about Him. He's not some mythical creature akin to Santa Claus waiting to give you everything on your Christmas list. No, He's a Father who loves His children. He is a Father who desires to give you an abundant life if you would just allow Him to give it to you. He has been chasing me and chasing you every day of our lives and its way past time we allowed Him to catch us.

I've never been to Divinity School, and I don't pretend to know everything as it relates to God or the Bible. I can do a better job of remembering the book and chapter numbers of scripture, but I can guarantee that if I tell you it's in there, it is. Google is an amazing tool and with just a few keystrokes, you can find the scripture I'm referencing. Besides you shouldn't just trust what I say or what your pastor says. Look the scripture up for yourself.

I don't know the Hebrew word that key words in the Bible derive from or how to pronounce many of the names or places mentioned within His book. But every day I live, I find that I learn more and more about God and what He desires for me. I've learned He is the best writer in the world because no one could have written my life's story as beautifully as He has. This season that I am currently in is unlike any I've ever experienced and I'm learning to have joy as I press my way through.

It's such an amazing experience for me that I want to share it with you. I want to share it because I think it's unfair for me to find the keys to freedom in Christ and not share them with you. As a matter of fact, I'm pretty sure He wants me to share. It is my sincerest prayer that before you get to the last page of this book that you have the most beautiful encounter with God. I pray that you are so enamored with Him that you crave not only time with Him but that you crave to hear His voice every day, multiple times a day. I pray that you understand the meaning of Let Go and Let God and in doing so, you find that the old saying "everything you need, you already have" is not just a familiar saying.

But you can't know my end without first knowing my beginning. Let's start with my introduction to Christ. Where you say? At church, of course!

CHAPTER 1

WHO ARE YOU AND WHERE DO YOU BELONG?

AME, COGIC, Baptist, Holiness, Protestant, Missionary Baptist, and so many more are just the beginning of the different denominations that exist in the world today. They all love the Lord but have their own belief systems and practices used to govern the body of Christ. Some feel women are only to serve in certain capacities in the church while others feel women should be free to serve however God leads them. There are those who feel morning service should be traditional with only the singing of hymns while others have a band complete with drums, keyboards and organs. Same God, different set of rules. Who's right? Who's wrong? I'm sure if you ask any one of them, they'll tell you they are the ones doing it right and everyone else should follow suit.

We have gotten so caught up in these traditions, guidelines and practices that we are missing out on one of the main things God wants us to focus on and that is relationship with Him. Our traditions are so ingrained in us that we find ourselves doing what our religion dictates and not what God commands. We don't intentionally leave God out, but we have convinced ourselves that by attending every church program and every church conference that we are in relationship with God therefore guaranteeing our little mansion in heaven.

It takes more than church attendance and singing in the choir to spend eternity with the Lord. Did you just gasp? Surely, you didn't think that just because you were nice to the people in the streets and showed up on Sunday, that your place in heaven was secured. You didn't think that because you attended church all your life and served in ministry that you were guaranteed an eternal life with God, did you? You can do all those things and still miss out on eternal life.

I grew up in church like many others. I had to be severely sick to miss church as church attendance, much like school attendance, was not an option. My family and I attended Sunday School and Vacation Bible School and Usher Anniversaries and Senior Choir Anniversaries and Revivals and everything else. If the doors were open, we were there. We would be in church until 2:00pm on Sunday afternoons only to return at 3:00 or 4:00 for a program. Not to mention we often stayed after church because my mama had meetings to attend or there was a person or two she needed to speak with before we could leave. I don't know that we ever went home directly after the benediction. Sundays, it seemed, was always the longest day of the week but it was our tradition and so we did no different.

And we didn't attend just any church. We attended our family church. It was the one my great grandmother attended. My grandfather was President and Lead Singer for the Gospel Choir. My grandmother, who answered the call to pastorship, served as Assistant Pastor. My family members served in many different capacities. Some sung in the choir, some ushered, some were on the Trustee's Board. On Easter Sundays, we had a speech. Christmas, another speech. Black History program, yet another speech. We were involved in all that the church had to offer. And we didn't dare think of leaving this church to join another. It didn't matter if our spiritual needs were being met or not. For a very long time, leaving was not an option. Truthfully, it was frowned upon so even today much of my family still attends that same church.

Our denomination came with traditions and practices, just like others, and we had to make sure we were always in compliance. Children were expected to take the long walk to the altar in front of God and everyone to give the pastor their hand and join the church by the age of 12. Communion was always to be held on the first Sunday. The missionaries were expected to be clothed in all white from head to two when assisting with Communion. Love Feast was observed on the fifth Sunday. Women were not allowed to wear pants. Shoulders and backs were to be fully covered. You were forbidden to step foot in the pulpit specifically where the pastor sat.

As kids we were expected to sit quiet during the service. We were to be seen but not heard. We did get to draw or write but one wrong move and an adult from somewhere would shoot you a look that could straightened you up with not even one word being spoken. The church mothers sat in one Amen Corner while the elderly men sat across from them in the other Amen Corner. There were so many rules both spoken and unspoken and we all followed them without question.

As a child and growing teenager, I never thought much about these traditions and practices. I followed them because that's what we were taught. I also never knew of a time in my life when I didn't know or believed in the Holy Trinity or more specifically Jesus. I've always known Him to be the Son of God. I've always known that He was born to the virgin Mary, was crucified, died and resurrected. I've always known that He died for our sins and His sacrifice granted us eternal life.

3

I learned about Adam and Eve, Noah and the Ark, Moses and the Red Sea, Jonah and the Whale and so many more Bible stories because I attended church. Even within the context of religion and tradition, I was given a foundation in Christ that I don't know I would have received had I not grown up in church. And while I received that foundation in church, I needed more to sustain me as I grew older. The Bible stories were cool. The scriptures were great. And the Sundays that offered the best singing were top notch. But the things I had learned were only scratching the surface of what I needed to know to live an abundant life and a life heavily entwined with Christ. I was receiving spiritual milk, but I needed to move to something solid. I needed to move from religious practice to relationship.

It was only when I grew older that I realized all churches didn't do some things the same. Imagine how shocked and confused I was to find that Communion could be served on any given Sunday. I will say I was a little taken back the first time I attended a church that observed it on the third Sunday. Did they not understand they were doing it wrong? And we didn't have to line up and take turns kneeling at the altar to take it? The pastor didn't have to hand everyone their wafer and juice independently? You mean to tell me we all had our own packets that we opened on our own and we all ate and drank at the same time? This had to be wrong because this was not what we were taught and not the way I had done in all my life. Was this way even sacred because initially it didn't feel the same? It took a moment for me to realize that Jesus couldn't care less what day we chose to observe the Last Supper. He said as often as you do this, do it in remembrance of me. We could have taken Communion on a random Tuesday for all He cared as long as we remembered His sacrifice.

I would have never thought about those traditions and my

upbringing had I not come to this season in my life. I knew what I knew, believed what I believed and as far as I was concerned, that was enough. God and I had grown from a place of me simply praying simple prayers to having conversations where I would speak, and He would listen and respond. Up until this point, I had never taken time to sit down and inventory my life. I had never really considered all that He had done for me but more importantly all that He had been to and for me. There were so many things He had done in my life daily that I had taken for granted.

In this new season, I began to look back at how my life had played out over 47 years and I recognized I was missing out on something I really needed. That something was deep intimacy with God. Up until this moment I thought I had it all figured out. My life had been great, but I was now at the point where I was realizing that all the things I considered great, were really small in the eyes of God. When you really begin to build a relationship with God you recognize that He wants to give you so much more.

For the longest time, I would proudly say that God was limitless in what He could do but I can admit that I did limit Him. Not only did I limit Him, but I also often worried how long He would allow me to live such an amazing life. He had already given me so much that I wondered if it were fair for me to want more. What if I did something to make Him mad? Would He take his favor away from me? What did I need to do to prevent that from happening? Would He really bring me this far in life to just take all His blessings away? In my spiritual mind, I knew He wasn't that type of God, but my flesh was saying something different.

If I had not found myself in this place, I am pretty sure I would have missed out on God's great blessings. Do you understand that your traditions and practices barely scratch the surface of who God is and who He wants to be in your life? Do you believe in an abundant life?

> *I am come that they might have life, and that they might have it more abundantly.* (John 10:10 KJV)

He wants us to have a full life. He wants us to have peace and joy. He wants us to delight in Him so He can give us the desires of our heart. Do you know why it is so easy for Him to give us those things we desire? It's because He is the one who places those desires in our hearts. I am not exaggerating when I tell you that God is amazing. I see it every day I live. I can truly say I am good even when it seems like life is falling down all around me.

Sometimes I sit on my porch and admire not just the beautiful flowers but the mesmerizing towering trees. Trees that don't require anything from us to grow because God sends the rain to water them for us. I take notice of the beautiful shades of red, orange and yellow foliage that form on the trees as Summer fades to Fall. I think of the calming oceans that smell and sound of tranquility as it softly soothes our souls. There is so much peace in His flowing waters. God has given us so much that we take for granted. We are so blessed in even the smallest things. He loves us enough to give us His very best.

While God is willing and wanting to give us more, He is requiring more from us. He wants to talk to us, spend time with us, come in and dine with us. I know it may be hard to think of communicating with someone you can't see but believe it or not, you do it every day! How you say? Read on! I have some secrets to share!

CHAPTER 2

YOU TALKING TO ME?

I began journaling at an early age although I didn't consider it journaling back then. Writing for me was therapeutic. It started out as a way to release my thoughts and energy. It was the way I chose to deal with life. As a young girl who didn't feel like she belonged or fit in, I needed to be able to talk to someone and express myself and there wasn't anyone. That's not to say I didn't have people who could be there for me and who would have wanted to be a listening ear, but I was not comfortable being vulnerable. I didn't want to be judged or ridiculed for my thoughts or feelings.

I'm sure I am not the only person who experienced these feelings growing up. You're in a normal, dysfunctional family feeling like somehow you were placed with the wrong people. Your family is the same as most families you know but somehow you just feel out of place. You feel like you don't fit. You spend your days trying to figure out if something is wrong with you until you finally realize God just made you different and that's okay. No two people were meant to be alike. But it's hard to wrap your mind around that thought when you're growing up. So I was that little girl who felt alone and needed an outlet and that's where writing came into play.

My writing wasn't always in a diary or a notebook. Many times it was just a plain sheet of notebook paper where I would write a letter to God or just write what I was dealing with that day. I eventually moved to a notebook and after writing I would carefully slide my notebook under my mattress. I would be devastated if anyone found and read my journal. I simply could not trust my thoughts and feelings in the hands of another person. I felt that if they knew how out of place I was feeling and if they read my thoughts and feelings, they would somehow use them as weapons against me and I wasn't willing to take that chance. That thought process followed me into adulthood and remains even now. I have an amazing husband, wonderful family and great friends but I am careful with the sharing of my thoughts and feelings. I am unable to be fully vulnerable with the people I trust the most.

While that has served me well in many situations it has also caused unnecessary anguish. It's hard for people to know how, what and when to pour into you when they don't even recognize that you are just pressing your way through life. That saying "Check on your strong friends, they are not okay" is a true statement. Problem is people like me will always tell you we're fine even when deep down inside we are struggling. We are careful to make sure our masks are on straight and that our countenance never slips. It's exhausting but for us it seems necessary.

I never gave thought to the fact that my writings were my prayers and way of communicating with God. When you grow up in religion you don't get a full understanding of intimacy in your personal prayers to God. You are taught the model Our Father Prayer at an early age and take pride in being able to recite it on command. When you wake up in the morning you get on your knees and say it and before you lay your head to pillow at night, you get on your knees and say it once more. At night you add a little razzle dazzle to it and add an extra line of "Now I lay me down to sleep". You may even take a few extra minutes to ask the Lord to bless certain people but you're just doing what you've been taught. You're following your denomination's blueprint with very little understanding. And it makes a lot of sense when you are little and innocent, and your biggest worry is if your mama is going to fix your hair in your favorite hairstyle the next day. But when you begin to grow up and endure failed friendships that you can't explain and bullying by people that you just want to like you, you find that you need more words.

Many of us, including me, didn't know how to form those words. We didn't know what we could say in our daily prayers to God. Were only certain words allowed? Did they have to go in a particular order? Were there certain words that got God's attention more than others? I didn't know the answer to any of those questions, but I did know I could write whatever I was feeling. And you know what, God answered. He responded. Sometimes He responded by the words that I would write following my words of frustration. They would be encouraging words of me telling myself I would be fine and to press on despite my frustrations. It would be me writing what my future would entail and that this too, whatever it was that day, would pass. God used my pencil to write what I needed to hear.

There were times when there were no encouraging words, but I would get up the next day feeling refreshed after a good night's rest and my day would be good. It would be a day of no bullying and the people I wanted to be friends with would choose me to be in their friend group that day. I would feel like I belonged and that was a good feeling. Who wouldn't want to belong? And although I knew it wouldn't last long, at least I had that day.

How else does God communicate? People in church would always say that God communicates to you through the Bible, His written Word and instructions for living. However, when I was growing up the only version of the Bible I remember is the King James version and what child could understand that? Truthfully how many adults can understand that version? The "thous" and "shalls" and "begots" were like a foreign language and many of the sentences didn't make sense in my mind. Later in life other versions such as the New King James, NIV, Messenger and Christian Standard, just to name a few, were created and the Bible became much easier to read and comprehend. I know there are many people who will say that these versions are just people trying to recreate the Bible to fit their own agenda. They feel like the only true written Word is the original King James version. My response to that is to compare what's written in your KJV to your newest translation. I guarantee they are essentially the same.

But with all that said, they were correct. God definitely communicates with us through the written Word. If you were to really take the time to read the Bible, you will find very similar stories of what we face today. There were evil people, wars, issues with the economy, adultery, singleness, fighting amongst family and the list goes on and on. But the Bible talks about how those issues were resolved or the methods put in place to have people cope with life whenever life was, well, lifeing. As the old saying goes, there is nothing new under the sun. And the same wisdom God shared then is useful and applies today.

You can't always wait for Sunday to roll around and hope that pastor addresses your issues. The answers are in the Book. "But what if I can't understand what it says?" Pray and ask God to make it plain for you. Ask Him to open your spiritual eyes so you can see and your spiritual ears so you can hear. Ask Him to put it in terms you can understand, and He will do it for you.

I know you may question where to start. The world of technology now gives you the option to Google, "what scripture should I read if

I'm dealing with depression" or whatever it is you have going on and it will give you some options. I've also found that if you pray and ask Him where to look, He'll answer. Case in point, a year before I met my husband, I was praying about wanting to get married and I asked God to give me an encouraging scripture. He took me to Isaiah 54:5 which reads: *For your Maker is your husband...*

It was funny then and it is funny now! He had made His point crystal clear! Once I read that verse, I changed my mind about finding a husband and started focusing on the husband I already had! It was a life changing moment. So much so that when a man did show up who would eventually become my husband, I didn't even want him. But that's a story for another book!

God communicates with us through others. No, this doesn't mean that everyone who walks up to you and says, "God told me to tell you", is really relaying a message from God. Sometimes people will play in your face if they don't think you know any better. You must be wise enough to know when it is really God sending a messenger to you to deliver a word or if the enemy is trying to throw you off track.

The first time I heard someone prophesy I was in awe. Think about it; a person, a lot of times someone you don't know, speaks to you and tells you something relevant about your life that they should not have any idea about. Suppose I came to you and said "God saw you last night as you sat on the edge of your bed crying. He wants you to know that all is well even though it doesn't seem like it. He is even now working on your behalf. He also wants you to know that He loves you and He meant it when He said He would never leave you or forsake you." Maybe you would think "Wow, He does see me, and He is listening" or "You mean to tell me He loves me so much that He sent someone to tell me that He is there even when I feel like He isn't." How could this stranger know where you were and what you were doing last night? Afterall this is the first meeting the two of you ever had and unless they were in the room with you or even in the house, they couldn't have known what occurred.

But God was there and He sent someone to tell you He still has your back. He is communicating to you audibly by using one of His other children to do so for Him. Let me tell you this, it's not only a blessing for the person on the receiving end of God's message; It's also a blessing for the person communicating the message. One, they had to have their spiritual ears open to hear from God. Second, they had to have such an intimate relationship with God that they not only knew He was speaking but felt comfortable enough to communicate it to a stranger without fear. And third, how awesome is it to be used by God for His glory?

Prophesy doesn't always have to be God responding to your prayers concerning life's challenges. Sometimes He sends people to tell you His plans for you. The first time that I can remember someone prophesying to me was at a small church in Dalton, GA. My friend Stephanie's brother-in-law was the pastor and this church had at most 20 total members. The prophet, whom I had never met, spoke to me and said, "There is healing in your hands." I walked away wondering if I was going to be the next Benny Hinn walking around laying my hands on people's forehead yelling "Healed!" Funny, I know. Now to be honest that doesn't mean that I won't do that, or I haven't done that however years later, God granted me revelation and said that the healing I had in my hands was through written word.

I've always loved to write and had been doing so in some form or fashion for years. Writing has always been my preferred method of communication and it was by far the way I best expressed myself. It was what I used to send beginning of the year messages to my friends telling them what I felt the new year was going to bring. It was what

I used to convey sweet messages to others to encourage them in their day. It was sometimes the way I chose to communicate my love to my children. I've always had a way with words as it relates to writing. I believe there are words I have written that have healed some hurts and anxiety in the lives of others. I believe the books I write using the words He gives me will offer answers to those seeking Him who are not sure what to do next. Yes, there is healing in my hands and God sent the prophet to tell me.

Think back over your life, if you will. Can you pinpoint a time when God sent someone to say something to you unexpected about your life? Maybe they walked up to you and said something as simple as, "I saw how you made that little boy laugh. Seems like you have a way with children. Have you ever considered being a teacher?" And unbeknownst to them you were just toying with the idea of going to school to be a teacher.

How about standing in the checkout line contemplating to yourself about purchasing a particular type of candy you've never seen before. You say to yourself, "I don't need that. It's probably not even good" only to have the person behind you say out of nowhere, "Have you ever had this candy? It's really good." How could they have possibly known you were thinking about that candy? They didn't and they didn't even realize they responded to your internal thoughts. They didn't even know or realize that God used them to communicate to you. I'm sure you're thinking that God is not concerned with those very small things in your life. Guess what? He is! He wants to know all about you and everyday He longs to hear from you even if it's to ask if you should buy a piece of candy. He looks for every opportunity to spend time with you. Why, you ask? Because He loves you! Duh! Besides it's not that deep. Religion, not relationship, told you that it was.

God also speaks to us through the Holy Spirit. In my early 20's

I attended my first and only Woman Thou Art Loosed conference in New Orleans, LA with my spiritual mother, Gloria. I met Gloria when I started working at Vickery Hall on the campus of Clemson University. Gloria, to me, was pure light and she was what I would call "saved saved". She did not play about God. She wasn't a pushy Christ follower, but she didn't shy away from who she was in the Lord. She was the type of person that you couldn't just say, "well I'll have to pray about that" because she would literally stop what she was doing and say, "Let's pray now. Go ahead." I couldn't tell her that was just something people said and not normally follow up on. If you said you were going to pray for something or about something she was going to make you do just that, even if you weren't ready. Trust me, it was a lesson I learned and caught on to very fast.

One of Gloria's ways of communicating with God was through the speaking of tongues. The only other person I had ever "known" to speak in tongues was Bishop TD Jakes. Every time I heard him give a sermon he would speak in tongues. His message wasn't in tongues, but he would speak it throughout his sermons almost like an exclamation in the middle of a sentence or similar to saying "Hallelujah" but with a heavier emphasis. It was a sacred language that gave off "anointed", "intimate", "connected". It was clear that God knew what he meant even if we didn't.

When he spoke in tongues, it never left me feeling confused. No, it left me with a desire to have the same connection with Christ that he had, but I thought that you had to have a certain status with God to have that type of anointing. Yes, I really, really wanted it but I didn't feel qualified.

Gloria and I were walking down the street to the stadium for one of the sessions when she began to speak in tongues. I thought she had said something to me that I didn't hear so I asked her to repeat what she said, and she responded, 'Oh I wasn't talking to you.

I was praying." She then continued to pray in tongues as if she was speaking English. I politely kept my mouth closed and wondered what I could do to have what she had and what Jakes had and what I was sure so many other people had. Was my relationship with God such that He would grant me this request? Could it be that, I too, qualified?

I don't remember ever asking Gloria about the baptism of the Holy Spirit, but God knew it was something I desired. Gloria and I went to her church the Sunday after the conference and wouldn't you know before the end of service one of the pastors asked if anyone there wanted to be prayed over to receive the baptism of the Holy Spirit and receive the gift of speaking in tongues. I could not get out of my chair quick enough. Inside I was screaming "Me! Me! Me!". I was anxious, excited and ready! I along with some others went to another room in the church and the people began praying for us in the Spirit. They were praying for us and had instructed us to pray for ourselves that we would receive the Baptism. The Spirit was high, as the older folks would say, and the Baptism happened and people who never spoke in tongues before began speaking and praising God. Everyone. But. Me. Okay, maybe I wasn't the only one but that's how I felt in that moment. It confirmed to me that I wasn't qualified for such an amazing gift.

Gloria, sensing my disappointment, encouraged me to continue to pray for it even after we left the church. She told me that speaking in tongues was a gift and that our Father loved giving us gifts. So even after I left Louisiana, I prayed for the Baptism of the Holy Spirit. My faith was probably the exact size of a mustard seed, but I was obedient and did what she said. And then it happened!

About two weeks later, I was about to walk downstairs from my bedroom to head to work when suddenly, my mouth opened, and words rushed out. Words I had never heard. Words I had never spoken. Words that to the natural ear made no sense but they were powerful, and they were flowing like a rushing river. I was excited, full and I could not keep still. It was everything I had imagined and more. It was indescribable and overwhelming. It was the Holy Spirit and He and God were communicating. I didn't then, and I don't even now, have the gift of interpretation of tongues; however, I can tell you there is a feeling that accompanies that language that lets you know what you are saying is being heard and understood in the Spirit Realm.

My speaking in tongues flows much like the English language complete with me asking questions and making non-verbal gestures. The Holy Spirit is interceding for me and having a conversation in the Spirit Realm that my carnal mind cannot comprehend. But my spirit understands. My emotions range from joyful to mournful depending on the conversation being had. I'd like to think that those conversations are about God's desires for me and placing those desires in my heart so that I can pray for them knowing that God would be overjoyed to give them to me. I'd also like to think the Holy Spirit is talking to God about those issues that I just can't seem to put into words but definitely need help with. Maybe there are requests to bless those I know and don't know, pleading on my behalf for them.

I imagine the Spirit is requesting grace, mercy and/or help that I haven't even thought to pray for on my own. He's advocating for me, and He and God are having a discussion. Do you have any idea how amazing it is to have someone advocate on your behalf? And that someone is not just anyone. He's part of the Trinity and He has been there before the world was created and He is taking the time to help me. Well, I guess that settles it. I definitely qualify and so do you! While I joke and say that I am God's favorite, I know you're

His favorite as well. He loves us all the same and just as He freely gave me gifts, He desires to do the same for you.

Knowing that God communicates with us through various means only made me want to hear more from Him. If He is thinking of me all the time, I would like to know what's on His mind. But I'm not selfish. I want to know what He thinks about you, too. My ability to hear from Him and share with you could be the difference between life and death. Literally! It could be the difference between eternal life and eternal damnation. Literally. What do I mean? Let's say you run into someone who is dealing with suicidal thoughts unbeknownst to you. Let's say when you see them, God lets you in on what's going on and He tells you to tell the person, "I know you are tired and you just want to give up, but God promises if you stick with Him, He'll bring light into your darkness. What you are dealing with, will pass!" Those few lines could be what changes a person's mind and pushes them to go through one more night only to find their situation beginning to change the next day. Had you not heard and not shared, that person could have chosen to give up.

Maybe a person is struggling with their belief in God. Maybe their child has unexpectedly passed away and they don't understand why. So, now they are mad at God, or they've decided they no longer wish to believe in God. Maybe in your conversation with them you say, "God knows you're mad at Him and He understands why. You wonder how a loving God could take your child away from you. But that same God gave His son so that we can have life again and although it hurts now you will see your child again. He understands your pain because He has endured the heartbreak of losing a child as well. He's still standing there with open arms and when you're ready to be comforted, He's more than happy to comfort you." That conversation can drive someone to have a much-needed conversation with God. He wants to wipe away all your tears, if you let Him.

What's next? Well, I have come to terms with the knowledge that God is communicating with me every day in some sort of way. Our relationship is growing but I still need more. We're several months from me leaving my job and I still have no prospects. I'm not seeing any action on His part. I have applied and been rejected for a job that I am more than qualified for with no real explanation. I have interviewed and been ghosted. I have even gone all the way to a final interview, which seemed very promising, only to be rejected.

I'm so confused. Again, I have been obedient. I have done what God has asked but now I see that I'm returning to my old ways. I'm spending less time in prayer and meditation. I know He's waiting to see and meet me in the morning but I'm no longer showing up at our meeting place and when I do choose to show, it's not at our agreed upon time. I know I didn't get the directions wrong, yet nothing's happening. My husband looks at me and asks in a joking manner if I can find another seat on the couch so as not to wear a hole in the one cushion I sit on daily. Lord, this is not the way I thought this was going to go. I was supposed to get time off, relax, go on my many pre-planned vacations, move my boys into college and be back to work in August. I'm stuck! But then my friend Donna calls.

During our conversation she mentions a book her Women's Group is reading and it changes my life. Remember I was listening to Micah sing about wanting another place in Him and wanting new levels and new dimensions? Remember Smokie was singing that I win even when the score says I lose? How about Tye telling me not to cry all night and all year because joy was coming? Well, this book was about to reveal how all of those things were about to happen and I could not be more excited.

CHAPTER 3

LISTEN AND OBEY

I've always wanted to prophesy and for many years I was able to do just that, but it has been years since I've operated in that gift. I know that God hasn't stopped talking to me. I just stopped listening. When He and I are in our secret place and it's just the two of us, it is very easy for me to hear Him. He has a way of giving me words and thoughts that I rush to put down on paper. It's always a sweet surprise to revisit my journal entries and find that God clued me in about His plans concerning me months before the events even began to unfold. The year before I met my husband, I wrote that I was living my last year single. I had no prospects, no longer cared if there was a prospect and really had no clue where to find a prospect! Clearly what I wrote was God's words and not my own.

Months before I applied to work for Mercury Industries, I wrote about the job I would have and how it would pay extremely well. I wrote that our financial situation was about to change for the better. I was offered the job and watched our salaries increase year after year after year. I simply wrote what I heard and felt just as I had always done. It's always easy to hear Him when things are still and settled but it's different when I leave my quiet place and re-enter the world. I find that the world is extremely noisy and when I choose to focus on what is being said and done in the world, the earthly realm, it's hard for me to hear what's being said in the spirit realm. The noise in the world is not like heavy traffic or children running and playing at a park but noisy like bills, decisions, too many people and everyday life. And sometimes it gets so noisy that I am consumed with all that I'm hearing that I can't quiet it all down long enough to stop to hear Him speak. Unfortunately, the last few years of my life have been extremely noisy.

Although I hadn't prophesied to anyone in years, it was a gift that I wanted restored. It was something I had been praying for off and on so when Donna told me the name of the book, I was all in and purchased it immediately. I found myself in tears after the first two chapters of the Prophetic Warrior. Author Emma Starks writes, "What God has put in me will change lives. I have been entrusted with weaponized gifts from the most powerful place in all of Heaven and earth." She wasn't just saying that about herself. She was saying that about me. She was saying that about you. God gives each of us gifts and we are to use those gifts to help build the kingdom of God. Her words were reminding me that I was not on this earth just for me but for others as well. My ability to give someone hope through prophesy could change their lives. My ability to have a relationship with Christ and share my testimony with others could bring others to Christ. God sent me to the world on assignment and He was requiring that I show up and perform as He commanded. I need you to understand that you were sent on assignment as well. But you must choose if you are going to choose His will or if you're going to choose your own.

She also wrote "We waste time seeking endless confirmation because we have lost the art of instant obedience, where we action what God says when He says it the *first time!*" Has God ever told you to do something or say something to someone for Him and instead of you being obedient, you start questioning God? "God, is that you? You want me to say what? To whom? But what if I'm wrong and they look at me weirdly? Okay, well if this is really you, let them walk my way because I need some type of confirmation." Instead of just being obedient and doing what God has instructed, we ask ten million questions in a quest to be sure it was Him speaking, only for us to miss the opportunity to share. Prophesying and speaking up is not easy. It should be though because not only is God asking us to deliver a message for Him, but He also expects us to be obedient. Instead, we get in our heads and start questioning Him.

I had a situation happen to me a few weeks ago where God gave me a message to share with someone in my gym class. I was toying with the thought that maybe the message given to me was from me and not from God. I said, "God, if this message is from you then no one will go up and start talking to her after class." For about 30 seconds no one approached her, so I proceeded to head her way only to notice someone was heading in the same direction. So what did I do? I walked away and rationalized that the message I was going to share was not from God. I then proceeded out of the gym and headed to my car. However, once I stepped outside the gym God kept pressing me to talk to wait and talk to her. Several times I attempted to just walk to my car but instead found myself turning around and returning to the sidewalk to wait. I figured she would come out and I could tell her then but after about 5 minutes of waiting, I decided she wasn't coming out and proceeded to my car. Yeah, I could always give her the message the following week, but what if it was something she desperately needed to hear that day. I had done just what Emma said. I asked for confirmation and was not obedient when God had already given me the message. How was it I had just been praying and asking God to restore my gift and use me as His instrument and not follow through on what He commanded? It was clear that I still had a lot of work that needed to be done.

Did I feel that because I failed to follow through with what God had commanded that He would not use me again? Of course not. God does not give us spiritual gifts to take them back. And although we are not always obedient, He does not give up on us. But I knew that just as I had prayed diligently for the Baptism of the Holy Spirit many years before, I would have to do the same for restoration. God needed to know He could trust me. He needed to know I was serious about being an instrument for Him. It's one thing to say it but it's another thing to live it.

Emma's book pushed me further into relationship with Christ. She reminded me that it wasn't just about showing up on Sunday and going through the motions. It wasn't about praying and watching God answer a prayer to then just go back and sit down on the sidelines. She forced me to face a very significant truth. What's that truth you ask? Because I was only seeking God in times of need and not working to deepen our intimacy, I was missing out on the true essence of who He was, who He is. I had allowed our relationship to become stagnant and routine. I knew when I called on Him, He would answer but He wanted more from me, and He deserved more than what I was giving. He was showing me just how insufficient I was on my own. There was and is nothing I can do outside of Him. In this season He was showing me that not only was He my Father, but He was also my very best Friend.

CHAPTER 4

HE'S A GOOD FATHER

I love my children immensely. There is nothing in this world that I would not do for them. My husband and I do our very best to provide for them. God has been so faithful as He has allowed us to give them everything they need and a whole lot of what they want. My children can never speak of a time where they were hungry or didn't receive something they requested. They have been good children all their lives, so we have never seen a reason to withhold things from them. It didn't matter if they asked for a PlayStation, Xbox, $300 sneakers, we were going to do whatever we could to make sure they received it. Our only request was that they were respectful to others, behaved and made good grades. As long as they stayed out of trouble and did what they were supposed to do, they could pretty much have anything they wanted. It delighted us to be able to do that for them. Them being happy made us happy. Our love for them has never known bounds and we would move heaven and earth to keep a smile on their faces.

Though for the most part they were great growing up, every now and again they would do something we were not pleased with, and we would have to discipline them. As children, that discipline could be a time out where they had to sit in their rooms alone for 5 or 10 minutes with no television so they could reflect on what they had done wrong. Sometimes they were prohibited from going outside and playing with the other kids in the neighborhood. Every now and then it was a pop on their hand or a spanking depending on the severity of their misdeeds.

In their teen years, we would take away their cell phones or game systems for a day or more which would force them to read which they found to be an undesirable task. (Like, how could anyone not love reading?!). Of course, if your family is like mine there is always that one kid who is super unbothered by any punishment given and would find a way to pass the time. Nevertheless, the discipline had to happen. A lesson needed to be learned and a change in behavior had to occur. Sometimes the discipline wasn't the taking away of something they cherished or restriction of some kind, but a simple conversation to address the behavior. Many times over the years they have said, "Mom, please. Not another life lesson!" It was never any fun for us to discipline them but we knew if they were to grow into law abiding, civic minded young men, we had to address the issues head-on and offer correction. And while they didn't like it, I can't remember them ever making the same mistakes twice, so I would say the discipline worked.

As they began to grow older, my worries for them began to change. In daycare and elementary school, they played with children of all races with no questions. What would happen when their eyes opened, and they began to see and experience racism? What would happen if they got to school and befriended a child who talked about sex and drugs because they saw and experienced it in their homes? How would this affect my children? I knew what they were being taught at home, but I couldn't be with them 24/7 and I couldn't control what others said to them. What about bullying and getting their drivers licenses and driving alone for the first time? What about depression and dating and trying to find their way in the world? The Lord had loaned them to us, and I wanted to make sure we parented them in a way that would be pleasing to God.

I used to say that I wish and wanted to shield them from life's adversities but then I realized my shielding them from the ugly world would not help them. They needed to experience whatever the world had to offer so that they would develop a need for Christ. He was the only person that would always be there for them 24/7. They needed to experience adversity so they could learn how to fight and press through life. They needed to experience adversity so they could realize that God could get them through anything if only they would trust Him. Life can drive you to Christ like nothing else can.

Why am I telling you these things? Because as I work on growing my relationship with God, I have received a very beautiful revelation. I know how full my heart is when it comes to my children. I would do anything in this world to keep them happy and at peace. There is no other love in this world that compares to the love I have for them. It's a powerful, unconditional, all-consuming love. My revelation? God's love for me is 10 times 10 times more than the love I have for my children! He feels the same way about you. He is our Father and He loves us so deeply that He wants us to live a good life. He wants the best for us. It is not His desire that we should suffer but when we choose our will over His, we are essentially asking for discipline. When we tell Him that our way is the best way, we are telling the Potter that He has no say in the making and shaping of the clay! He is our Creator, and He has every right to tell us what to do. It is His pleasure to bless us and grant us our heart's desire, but He will respond in loving discipline when we decide we know what's best for us. How do I know? Well, let's just say He has taught me some long, hard but much needed, lessons.

I was working for a fairly decent company and earning above

average wages. It was chaotic at times but I always say I do my best work in chaos. My manager quit in the middle of the day and her manager asked if I would fill in until they found a replacement. I said sure and was happy to keep the site going. When the position was posted, I applied as I knew I was more than capable of performing the job. The job remained vacant for over a year and I continued to perform in an interim capacity. However, when the company began interviewing to fill the position, I wasn't afforded the opportunity to interview, and they chose to hire an external candidate.

He was the opposite gender and race of me, but I decided I would not dwell on that fact and would just back up to my actual position and do the job I was hired for initially. Although this new hire was nice and not a problem to work for, I quickly realized he was fine taking a back seat and allowing me to run the site as I had done before his hire. This upset me greatly. He had the title and the pay that they didn't feel I was ready for, yet he wanted me to continue to do the job. Well, I had made up my mind that I wasn't going to continue in that role. Mind you, I said I had made up in my mind what I was going to do. What about what God wanted me to do?

I had prayed about my situation, and I had determined that God wanted me to find a new employer. So that's exactly what I did. I found another job! I did not feel good about the job or the company from the beginning. I had to keep calling and following up for months after my interview to find out my hiring status. I wasn't smart enough or in tuned enough to realize that God was providing me a way out. If they wanted me for the job, they would be calling me and making me an offer and not the other way around. They would be chasing me because they didn't want to lose me to another company. But I didn't take God's hint. I just kept calling and inquiring and pressing the issue until they finally offered me the position.

This new position was going to pay more money but my drive to work would increase to 30 minutes as opposed to the 15-minute commute I currently had. And because I was further away from home, I couldn't drop in and have lunch with my kids at school or volunteer to do things with their classes. I loved being a salaried employee because it gave me an opportunity to be more present with my kids as school, which was something my single parent mother wasn't able to do. Yes, their dad was available, but I wanted to be there sometimes, too. I didn't want to put a lot of extra miles on my car, so we purchased another vehicle. There went that raise in pay! And to top it all off, I hated the job. It was too quiet. No one needed me for anything. I was hired because they had to have someone in that role, but they didn't really take the position seriously. The work demographic was 95% male and there was so much drama it felt like being a supporting cast member of a soap opera. The company had no rules, so people just did what they wanted to do without consequences, and did I mention that I hated it?

God was teaching me a great lesson. I moved before He told me to move. And I went somewhere He didn't direct me to go. He was blocking me from what He knew would be an unpleasant experience, and I was choosing to go around Him. And I knew it! I knew it before I signed the offer letter. I knew it when I was giving my two weeks' notice. But I did it anyway and He moved out of the way and gave me what I wanted. How long did He allow me to learn my lesson? Four very long years. I really should have listened.

Did God still love me when I decided to go with my will instead of His? Absolutely. But He had to show me what happens when I think I know more than Him. Had I just waited on Him, I wouldn't have had to suffer that long. Had I been obedient and just endured until He said it was time to go, I could have spent the time I wanted with my children when they were in elementary school. I wouldn't have had to purchase another car ensuring not just an additional car payment but an increase in car insurance. This was a case of "I can show you better than I can tell you. You want it? You can have it." He allowed me to do what I wanted and because I was a 'Miss Know It All", I got to suffer until I fully learned my lesson. Did I get paid well? Yes, but I would have gladly given that back to have the freedom I had before. My peace is worth more than any amount of money. And there is no price you can put on obedience.

See if I had taken our relationship seriously and understood who He was and what He was doing, I would have known the best thing for me was to do what He said. He gave me so many chances to get out of what He knew was going to be a bad situation for me, but I was determined to do what I wanted and so He relented and allowed me to make the mistake. So, I got what I got! I bet if you were to stop for a moment, you could think of many times God told you not to do something and you did it anyway. You did it because you thought you knew best. You prayed and asked Him what to do but when you received an answer that you didn't like, you just kept praying and said, "God hasn't answered me, yet." Yes, He did! You just didn't like His answer, so you pretended you didn't hear Him. And then when you did what you did, which was what you wanted, and it didn't work out, you went back to Him and asked Him to get you out. And after He let you suffer for a while and after you learned your lesson, He brought you right on out. Guess what? You're in good company. We are all some hard-headed, stubborn children! I'm so glad He still loves us even when we are disobedient.

This deeper relationship that God and I are developing has given me new insight. You see, I like working. I have worked in Human Resources for over 20 years, and I felt like my job was in many ways, my ministry. I was the ear and the shoulder for many people. I offered solace and encouraging words to those who needed it. I disciplined when required but I always did my best to lead with love and compassion. Somedays it was a lot, overwhelming even, but I genuinely loved what I did, and I enjoyed helping people.

While I had experienced a lot at all the companies I had worked for, none compared to my time at Mercury Industries. Over a span of 9 years, we had buried 10 team members, endured the COVID pandemic, terminated beloved co-workers due to restructuring and although it was draining, it was fulfilling. Now I had walked away from that and though I was obedient, I was struggling. As much as I knew and trusted God, I was not allowing Him to operate fully in who He was. The only way to do that was to work on this relationship of ours and move out of the way so He could lead. I had no other choice. Life had pushed me right to where He desired and destined me to be. And that was in His hands. I had to put away everything that made sense to me and just allow Him to complete His plan.

Looking at my life, things just didn't make sense. How could he tell me to leave my job and my stable compensation and then allow all these hardships to follow? It seemed like as soon as I walked away, trouble began coming from every side. I didn't understand. How could this be the result of obedience? The math wasn't mathing. But now that He and I were talking on a more intimate level, the pieces of the puzzle began to fall into place. He needed to get the glory out of this season in my life. The only way to make that happen was to allow me to walk in a season that looked impossible to the world.

Imagine the testimony I would be able to share with others? Imagine how many people would hear my story and decide to be obedient to the voice of God? All of this was for His glory! He had already asked me time and time again if I trusted Him. Now He was asking me if I had faith in Him.

CHAPTER 5

HE WANTS COMPLETE CONTROL

I love to read and have been known to pick up random books in Christian bookstores in hopes of reading them at some point. I am not sure where I picked up this particular book, but God knew it was a book I needed to read. Recognizing the Spirits that Hinder the flow of God by Pastor Jim Bolin was a rare find. Pastor Bolin uses the river as a metaphor to illustrate how God's blessings for us flows like a river of abundance. And although he uses the river to explain blessings, I see how that same metaphor could be used to explain our faith and how an increase in faith can lead to an abundance of God's blessings.

Let's take a journey to the river of faith. Picture yourself walking out into the river and the water is around your ankles. Are you comfortable in the river? Well, who wouldn't be comfortable with ankle deep water, so the answer is probably yes. Now go a little deeper into the river where the water is now around your waist. Are you still comfortable? Hmmm, probably not as comfortable as you were when it was around your ankles, but I think we could all agree that in calm waters, we would be comfortable in waist deep water. But it doesn't stop there. Go out even deeper where the water now comes up to your neck. How are you feeling now? Personally,

I'd rather go back to the ankle-deep water because at least I have some control. I can simply get out if things get too rough. Finally, I need you to lay down and float in the river and allow it to take you wherever it chooses. Would that be comfortable for you? (Insert wide eye emoji right about here!). Let me put it all in perspective.

Jesus is the river. He is the Living Water. Many of us are comfortable being ankle deep in Jesus because although we like having Him around, we like to be in control. We also like that we can walk in or out when we choose. Today, I'm following what God says but tomorrow it's what I want. Today, I'm quoting scripture on social media but tomorrow I'm back to cussing folks out. It's easy to go back and forth when it's only ankle deep. But the deeper you walk into the water, the less control and decision-making ability you have and that's uncomfortable. Even at neck deep you can still just walk out and take back your control. It may not be totally comfortable but it's doable. However, the moment you choose to lay down in the water and give it ALL control, you find that you can't just get up and walk out whenever you desire. No, the further into the water you go, the deeper it gets, and standing is no longer an option. You find that you have no other choice but to let go and go wherever the river takes you.

The thing about the river is it's unpredictable. A storm can come through at any time and suddenly, without warning, the waters are choppy and rough and no longer calm. The river glides over sand and rocks and waterfalls and because you're trusting the river, you must go wherever it takes you. It knows what it's doing, and it knows where it's leading even when you don't know. You see, the moment you decide you're going to go deeper into the water and the moment you choose to lay down and float, you are telling the Lord that you're along for the ride with Him wherever it may lead. Wherever He is, is where you want to be. And you trust that regardless of what comes your way He is in complete control and will take care of you. You are allowing Him carte blanche over your life. And that, my friend, takes an enormous amount of faith. I'm not talking mustard seed faith. I'm talking "I Surrender All" faith. I'm talking "God Faith". Are you ready to float? Do you have enough faith to let Him take you wherever He chooses?

I have discovered a deep love and trust for Him that is showing me how to float in this figurative river. In some ways I was forced into this river and I'm okay with that. If it were not for this situation, I don't know that I ever would have gotten to this point. Then again maybe I would have, but at a much later date therefore missing out on some great blessings on the way. I would not have been able to experience this type of faith. I believe there is purpose in all things and maybe this is just one of the many lessons He desired for me to learn.

Going to work and earning a paycheck was me being in ankle deep water. When the environment became toxic, I walked out a little deeper, but I was still comfortable and somewhat in control. My company had no reason to get rid of me. My performance reviews were always great, and people liked me. My personality drew people. I would venture to say, the Light that shone within me, was a magnet and so people sought me out. Sure, there were things I could improve on but nothing that would make someone want to terminate my employment.

Mercury Industries was the fourth company I had worked for, and I always told myself I would never be fired from there or anywhere else. Me no longer working for any company would be a choice I made for myself. No one else had the authority to fire me. I would always say I was Captain of my ship and God was Master of my soul. I'm pretty sure that's not how the actual saying goes but my point was God was always in control and so no man had the right to dismiss me from any job God gave me.

I found myself neck deep in this water and God was asking me to make a choice. They told me they really wanted me to stay on with the company and apologized for what had transpired but God was calling me to float and though I trusted Him, I was afraid. It would be easier for me if I could just stand there and deal with what I could see. He would still help me, wouldn't He? Could I walk out a little further and still maintain some control? I mean I could just walk away, take the summer off and start working in the fall. I would still be good, right? Yeah, I had a plan. But my plan wasn't His plan. I thought God was going to lead me to calmer waters. Instead, He led me out into the deep where I had no other choice but to lay down.

What do you do when you find yourself floating with no clue where you're headed? Again, please understand that I thought I had it all worked out. With my credentials, there was no way I wouldn't be able to find a job and I should be able to find one whenever I was ready. I wasn't overly concerned about the initial compensation because God gave provisions. But when my plans fell through and nothing I planned came into play, I begin to panic. As sad as it may sound, Him continuing to say, "Do you trust Me?" was good but it was not enough. I needed more. I wasn't going to tell anyone I was struggling. I was going to continue to smile and say I was good. And for the most part, I really was, but some days were harder than others. Then I started to notice God was sending me messages to comfort and encourage me. And He was sending them through social media. That's right, good ole Tic Toc!

Yes, you read that correctly. I "discovered" Tic Tok sometime in 2022 and it was becoming one of my favorite past times. People are interesting and many of the Creators' content would catch my attention. You can find almost anything on Tic Tok. People dancing, clips from old television shows, people pranking each other, skits, jokes, sports, churches and politics just to name a few. If you can think of a subject, best believe it can be found on Tic Tok. I messed around and found church Tic Tok and for the most part that is what began to flood my FYP or For You Page for those of you who are new to this. Don't worry, I didn't know what it was until my teenager enlightened me. (Teenagers are quite useful!)

As I scrolled through the app, I found that every other video was someone telling me to trust God in this season. I had people telling me to stop scrolling because they wanted to pray for me, and their prayer would always be relevant to my current circumstance. They told me to keep going and to trust where God was leading. They wanted me to understand that even in that moment, God was working on my behalf. They were saying, without saying, stay in the water and trust the water to take care of you. Now, I'm smart enough to know that a plethora of people saw the exact same videos that I saw. But for me they were confirmation.

Tic Tok also introduced me to a Creator named Tee White, a single mother of two. Her spirit really resonated with mine and many times I thought to myself, "this is a woman I could be friends with if we lived closer!" She and I have never met but she utilized her platform in a way that you would think she was having conversations with her friends. Tee had a very successful career, but she recognized she did not have the work/life balance she wanted so she, too, had chosen to walk away. She had prayed and sought counsel with her mother and concluded that she needed to resign from her job. I'm not sure if she had a plan but she knew she could not continue taking time away from her children, so she did what she felt she had to do. Little did she know, walking away from her job would open her up to something or should I say, someone unexpected.

Tee talks about how she had given up on dating and was not

looking or expecting to find someone when a random person sent her a text inquiring if she was still single. While her response was not the sweetest, it kept the conversation going and that conversation led to a date. Tee has not stopped smiling since this first date. She lights up when she talks about this new man in her life. Her smile is so contagious and her voice so full of sunshine that people often comment on how happy she is and how happy they are to see her in this space. Had she not walked away from her job, she would not have had time for this new love God wanted to send her. He had to move the obstacle to bring her the blessing. And I know God will restore to her all and more than she had before, but a detour needed to happen on her way to destiny.

Her story is encouraging. Although we are on different paths, we both chose to be obedient. Our Father, Our Friend, wanted us to know that He is always in control. All we have to do is continue to trust and have faith in Him. In His time, He will prove Himself to be faithful. He has consistently whispered in my ear from the time I was a little girl until even now, that He was going to blow my mind and bless me pass my imagination. Well, the time has come. He has work for me to do. I must fulfill my destiny.

CHAPTER 6

I'M HIS

My mother has 4 children. If we were to go to Paternity Court to determine if we were truly siblings, Judge Lauren Lake would tell us the percentage of our relatability is 99.9999%. How would she know? As the old folks say, DANA don't lie. DANA is DNA's nickname. DNA according to Oxford Languages is "the carrier of genetic information." You want to know your genealogical lineage? You want to know your family history? Order you a kit from AncestryDNA or 23andMe or one of the other many providers. All you have to do is put your saliva sample in the tube they send you and send it back to them. They will then use genetic testing to determine if there is familial relationship between you and others in their database. Once they have determined those possible matches, they give you access to that information along with other reports they have available. It's all quite interesting.

That DNA is specific to who we are related to in the human race. If you are adopted and looking for your birth family, this could be a great service. If you simply want to know what area of the world your family originated from, these tests can be used for that as well. However, there is another determination of family that requires no testing. You don't have to be tested because who you are is already written and was written before you were even a thought in your mother's mind or an embryo in her womb. What's that you ask? Your spiritual DNA. It's what God has given us to let us know not only that we are all related but that we all originate from the same Father.

Go back to the book of Genesis and read how God created the world. I want you to specifically look at Genesis 2:7. It reads: *Then the Lord God formed a man from the dust from the of the ground and breathed into his nostrils the breath of life, and the man became a living being."* Did you catch that? I'm sure you already knew that verse but really lean it to what it's saying. Man was not alive until God breathed the breath of life into his nostrils. When you give a person CPR, you have two tasks to perform depending on the situation. If the person's heart is not beating, you apply chest compressions. But if you find that the person is also not breathing, you administer mouth-to-mouth resuscitation. You are essentially breathing life back into the person. You become a human ventilator until the person is hopefully able to resume breathing on their own. Adam was not breathing. He didn't even have a breath of his own to resume. So, when God breathed into him, into his body, into his lungs, not only did He bring him to life, His breath, His Spirit is what sustained Adam.

I'm sure you're wondering about Eve. God didn't breathe life into her nostrils so does she have the Spirit of God within her as well? She most certainly does! When God began to create Eve, He caused Adam to fall into a deep sleep. As he slept, God removed one of his ribs and used it to make woman-Eve. When God presented Eve to Adam, Adam said, *"This is now bone of my bones and flesh of my flesh; she shall be called "woman" for she was taken out of man.* (Genesis 2:23). Eve was created from Adam. She was taken from him. This means whatever he had, she had also. Therefore, God is in her DNA as well. And that DNA has continued to flow and is now present in each of us. The same Spirit that lived in Adam and Eve lives in us. God told them to be fruitful and multiply. Every time they procreated, they brought forth yet someone else with God's Spirit. And that Spirit has continued down the line to you and me and will continue with our children and our children's children.

We house inside our earthly bodies the Spirit of God. When someone says, "Everything you need, you already have", they are referring to the Spirit of God. What's greater than that? Within you lives the One who created the heaven and the earth and all that lies within. You know the scripture that says, *"Because the one who is in you is greater than the one who is in the world"* (1 John 4:4)? We have the "Greater" and everywhere we go, He goes. It doesn't matter if you're sitting at a ball game or in church on Sunday, He is right there with you. Regardless of what the enemy throws your way, you have what you need to defeat him.

He's not unaware of who your Father is and all He can do but he's counting on you being unaware and not remembering. He's hoping that when you get up in the morning that you forget to put on your weapons of warfare. He's hoping that you focus on waring in the carnal and forgetting that our warfare is really happening in the Spirit Realm. He's hoping you focus on the person or persons being used to hurt you. He wants you to get mad and say mean and evil things instead of asking God to give you the words to say to stop the arrows being thrown at you. He loves to stir things up and he gets excited when you take your focus off God and turn your attention to your problems.

If he can get you wrapped up enough in the world, you'll forget all about your Father and the power and authority He possess therefore forgetting the power and authority you possess. You'll come up with your own solutions and not even think to talk it over with your Father. And when the prince of darkness feels he has you right where he wants you, he'll leave you there in turmoil as he smiles signifying his satisfaction with his work. I need you to know that the battle is already won. Satan has already been defeated. When he shoots fiery darts at you, don't try to defend yourself against the darts. Go after the one who is shooting them at you! How do you do that? With the Word of God. *Submit yourselves, then, to God. Resist the devil, and he will flee from you!* (James 4:7). God's Words are your weapon and anytime you level them at the devil, he has no choice but to leave you alone. Darkness cannot comprehend light. If you walk into a dark room and you flip the switch, the room is going to light up. Satan is the prince of darkness and when the Light shows up, he has no other choice but to go away. The Light lives in you! Everything you need, you already have!

Speaking of Spirit, one of my favorite scriptures is Jeremiah 1:5, *"Before I formed you in the womb I knew you, before you were born, I set you apart."* There is another part of this scripture that refers to God appointing Jeremiah as a prophet to the nations, but I want to focus on the first part. Do you think Jeremiah was the only person that God knew before being formed in the womb? I used to say that this was one of my favorite scriptures because although God knew I wouldn't be perfect, that I would make many mistakes, He still decided He wanted me on this side of heaven. Not only did He know He wanted me here, He had a set time for my arrival. He knew what family I would be born into, and He knew how I would fit into that dynamic. He knew what hardships I would endure, and He knew how I would respond to those hardships. But more importantly He sent me here for a reason. He sent me with purpose. He sent you with purpose.

We all at some point in life struggle with knowing what our purpose is but I can assure you, you have one. Yes, we were sent to worship and adore Him but that's not the only reason we were sent.

There is indeed more. He is willing and wanting to tell you what that more is that He has planned for you. You need to go deeper into relationship with Him. You need to listen to what He has to say. And you need to wait for His timing. Trust me, there are no coincidences and there is a purpose for everything. Block out the noise and hear what He's trying to tell you.

Back in the early part of 2020, I was scheduled to have part of my thyroid removed. My thyroid was enlarged and after several ultrasounds and a couple of biopsies it was determined that there was a 50% chance I had thyroid cancer. The only option was to have the half with the suspicious nodules removed. My husband and I were joined by mother and sister at the hospital the day I was scheduled for outpatient surgery. The surgeon did an amazing job and after staying one night in the area, my husband and I traveled back home. About a week later the surgeon called and confirmed that it was indeed cancer, but it was small, and he got it all so nothing else needed to be done. Praise the Lord! Recovery was relatively easy and other than my body trying to figure out what was removed, I was in good shape and returned to work a week later.

Some several months passed when I got a call from my friend, Donna. There was someone at her church who was going to be having the same surgery. The young lady was very nervous about the procedure and subsequent recovery. Donna asked me if I would mind speaking with her to hopefully put her mind at ease. I said, yes, of course and Donna passed on my number to her so she could call when she was ready. When I spoke with the lady, she filled me in on why she was needing surgery and explained to me why she was nervous. While our situations were not exactly the same there were enough similarities for me to offer her some comforting words. I talked her through my surgery, told her how well the surgery and recovery went, encouraged her, told her I would be praying for her and told her all would be well.

Weeks later after she had the surgery, I reached out to see how things had gone and just as I told her, everything went well. My thyroid cancer in my opinion, was a non-event. I wasn't worried about the outcome as I knew God already had it under control. But I was glad that I had the experience because it gave me the opportunity to not only show God's love to a stranger but to give Him glory because we both were healed. Just like my story helped her, I'm sure her story will help someone else. The thyroid cancer had purpose.

CHAPTER 7

HE'S ALWAYS KNOWN YOU

I've never thought heavily about the Spirit Realm until Emma Starks discussed it in Prophetic Warriors. She discussed how our ability to see and hear God in the Spirit Realm fed into our gift of prophesy. When I read that, I began to wonder if I had ever had that experience. I truly wondered if I had ever spent time there and if I had, what did I need to do to get back to that place? Not just what was required to get back but was I really ready for that experience.

As I began to think on that I started to remember the future events that I had written down in my journal when God placed the thoughts in my spirit. Remember I started this book by telling you I wrote two months prior to leaving Mercury Industries that I would be leaving the company. How did I know that if God hadn't told me? I liked my company so why would I want to leave. I also thought about various scenes from my life that played out in my mind months or even years before they ever came to pass. When I would have those visions, I would just smile to myself and say that sometimes God is kind enough to give us glimpses of what's to come. I never attributed the hearing or seeing of those events as me spending time in the Spirit Realm. But the only way I could know that those events were going to happen was to have had seen or heard them outside of the natural realm. The world has no idea of what's to come in my life. Only God knows those details. As the writer of my life's story, He knows what's going to happen before it happens.

This got me to thinking a lot of thoughts that I wasn't sure I was ready to explore. Donald Lawrence's song *Spiritual* says, *"You're not a natural being having a spiritual experience. But you are a spiritual being having a natural experience."* I've always liked the song even though I was clueless about the meaning of the words they were singing. How could I be a spiritual being having a natural experience? But then I read Emma's book, and she says, "Man is essentially spirit." Now I'm forced to really think about the meaning of what they both have said.

Suddenly God takes me back to the scripture in Jeremiah. Remember God said, "Before I formed you in the womb, I knew you." I am now curious as to when He knew me. Where was I before I entered my mother's womb? Is it possible that God knew me in the Spirit Realm before sending me to the earth? If He knew me before I was formed in the womb, that means I already existed and when the appointed time had come, He sent me to earth. And He didn't send me because He was sitting there bored. He sent me because there was work for me to do. It's amazing how much He has shown me since I stopped running and allowed Him to catch me. All He has wanted was a deeper more meaningful relationship with me so I could get to know Him better. He wants to share His plans for my life with me. He desires a deeper relationship with you, too. He has so much to tell you.

For the first twenty years of my adult life, I worked in industry. My work in industry didn't take away the knowledge I had of God's will for my life. I've always known that He had great plans for me. I just didn't know how He planned to accomplish these plans. You know it's never the ending that is concerning, it's the process to get to the end. You are pretty certain that in the end of a thing, you're going to be victorious but the path to the finish line is bumpy and curvy and can cause anxiety. No matter what obstacles I have faced in life, I always knew in the end I would be okay. I always knew that things would work out just fine. These obstacles I faced showed up in many ways. Sometimes they were within my health or the health of a loved one. Sometimes it was in my finances. Sometimes they showed up on my job. But regardless of what showed up and when it showed up, I could always say God was in control and that everything would work out for my good. I just often found myself, like many others, struggling on the way to "all is well". And just when I would feel I could not take anymore, the sun would shine again and all the rain that proceeded the sunshine would be forgotten.

Here I was 4 months out from walking away from my job and I was struggling on the path to victory. But God created a very noticeable shift in my life. He reminded me of something He told me when I first started working at Mercury Industries. He knew how excited I was when I started working there. I felt valued and needed again and I was establishing an identity for myself and my department. I went to work joyous every day. It had been a long time since I had been happy going to work and this place was doing it for me. I remember one day my husband commented that this was the first job that I had not complained about and while he was happy for me, he was also surprised. I told him I didn't complain because I liked it there! But one day when I was thinking about how great it was, God spoke to me and told me I wouldn't be there forever. After working for three other companies, I was excited about the possibility of retiring from Mercury Industries. Yet here God was telling me that was not going to happen. I didn't want to hear or believe that, so I promptly dismissed the thought right out of my head. It was only when I walked away for the last time that he reminded me of what He had said years prior.

God already had a plan for my future that didn't involve me retiring with this company. He had shown me many years before in the Spirit what I would be doing in the latter years of my life, but I made excuses as to why that life would never exist for me. I knew I would write books, but I started several times only to quit. I had one book that I spent a lot of time on and felt really good about, but I let someone read it and they critiqued it so bad that I abandoned the book all together. It was only later in life that God spoke to me and told me that everything isn't for everybody. God never directed me to have that person proofread the book. That was a decision I made on my own. I never considered the fact that the person may not be able to receive what was written because the subject was not something they had experienced.

You ever started reading a book only to find yourself uninterested in the content, so you put it back on the shelf? Then months or even years later, you pull that same book back off the shelf to give it one more chance. The first time you tried to read it, the story or the subject didn't resonate with you, so you found it boring and chose to leave it alone. But after a while life tossed you into some situations and now this book that you once placed on the shelf is giving you solutions to your problems. I've had that experience several times. I begin reading a book only to put it back because it's boring. But then something in life draws me back to that same book and now it's like a glass of water to a thirsty man! I offered spiritual food to someone who did not have a craving for it, so he politely declined. I took that as a sign that no one would want to read what I had written and so I abandoned the book. Instead of listening to God, I chose to listen to man. I chose to be disobedient.

What did I learn? I learned to stop letting man dictate my

future. If God has already given me the plan and He is providing the necessary provisions, my desire should be to please Him and Him only. If He put the desire in my heart, He's going to come through and make sure I receive that for which I asked. Before He formed me, He made plans for me, and it is not up to me to change those plans. What *is* up to me is taking the time to meet Him in the Spirit to hear and see what He has planned. I am then not to question the plan, regardless of what it looks or even feels like, but to trust where the Spirit is leading me. Truth of the matter is, had God not allowed the situations at work to happen, I would still be there. And once again I would be choosing my will over His. And His will is so much better than mine!

CHAPTER 8

FINISHING WHAT HE STARTED

Shift happens. Say it very slow so you don't mess up. Shift. Happens. I've heard of shifting and I'm sure there were many times in life where I shifted in some form or fashion. But in this season, I not only feel the shift, I also see it. What do I mean? I told you in a previous chapter that I liked working and wanted to get back to work but nothing was working in my favor. I changed up my routine a little bit and I started adding gym time to my schedule. Everything in life was beginning to flow. I would get up and have my prayer and devotion time, watch a little television and then head to the gym.

As I began reading Prophetic Warrior my craving for writing came back. I had prayed about writing a book many times after my last abandoned project, but I really had not done much more than pray. But now I really, really wanted to start a new book. I had purchased an Apple MacBook months before for no reason, at least that's what I thought, so I had no excuse for not writing. My children were off at college and my husband was at work, so I had nothing but quiet time in the evenings. I now had a full day that started at 8:30 rather than 5:30 and though it lasted later into the night, I enjoyed getting on my laptop and just writing what God placed on my heart. But I was hard on myself. What if the words I typed were Trina inspired and not God inspired? I wasn't writing for the fun of writing. My prayer was for at least one person's life to be changed after reading my book. My hope was that someone would see themselves in at least one of my stories and it would drive them to the arms of Jesus. That would be most wonderful and fulfilling.

Not only was I drawn back to writing, but I was also starting to lose my desire for Human Resources, and I was starting to not want a traditional 8-5 job. I liked the life I was living. I started to think that the reason I wasn't getting called back or moving towards any job offers was because God was ready to start a new thing in me. Better yet, He was completing what He started. I would see jobs posted but there would not be any motivation to apply. I wasn't quite sure how this all was supposed to work but God was leading me away from the work life I had known for 20 years and placing me on another path.

I now have this book that is pushing me deeper and deeper into relationship with God and on top of that I'm questioning my future. I know I'm supposed to be writing but I don't know if what I'm writing is good enough. I'm kind of sure I'm on the right track but I'm also confused. Then my husband randomly calls me on the phone. He's headed south to see his mom and calls to chit chat. He questions me about my daily schedule because in his mind I'm not being productive. He talks about what my day looked like when I worked compared to what it currently looked like. He was concerned that I might be becoming depressed and complacent, and he knew that wasn't me. Then the Lord used him to speak to me and when he spoke, my jaw dropped.

You want to know what he said? He said, "Trina, you should be writing a book." Whoa! Where did that come from? Whenever he would call to check on me in the evenings, he would always ask what I was doing. My response was always either "nothing" or 'watching television". I never once told him that I had already started on a book. When he told me that's what I should be doing I went ahead and brought him up to speed and let him know I had already started. He then said, "Let me offer you some advice on writing this book." I'm going to be honest. When he said this to me, I rolled my eyes and thought to myself, "What kind of advice can a person who's never written a book give me about writing a book?" Remember I said that to myself. God wouldn't allow me to make that snide remark out loud, so I just continued to listen. He then said, "Just write. You can put it all into perspective later." And those words made all the difference in the world to me. I had been so focused on making sure my book was perfect that I failed to remember my book was God ordained and that, in and of itself, made it perfect. I was simply typing what He laid upon my heart, so it didn't have to be perfect to me. It only needed to be perfect to Him.

There was one last thing that he said that was further confirmation to me. He said, "Next year when it's time for you to go back to work, I want you to be able to say, "I don't want to go back" and I'll support you all the way." God had given provision to allow me the time to have my book written and in stores and online way before I needed to return to work. I had never considered not going back to work and here God was telling me if I continued to trust Him, I wouldn't have to step foot in anyone else's plant. He had other places He needed me to set foot in for Him. Had God not blocked those jobs, I don't know that this book and the ones to follow would have ever happen. God writes the absolute best stories!

God also sent confirmation through my friend, Shonda. On my birthday, she texted these words to me, "*Praying that this season of new beginning that God perfectly orchestrated brings you continued peace, joy, love, fulfilment, and new experiences that exceeds even your wildest imagination.*" How could she have known that I was experiencing revelation on God's direction for my life? How could she had known that I was about to embark on something new? Yet here she was telling me it was all perfectly orchestrated by God, and I knew she couldn't be more right. She and I hadn't talked in months, so she had no idea what I was currently experiencing yet her words were so on time, so comforting, and so prophetic. Weeks later while we were randomly texting, she told me that before she sent that text God told her this was my season of "newness." She then proceeded to ask me about my book. She said God told her to ask me where it was. Aside from my husband, our friend Donna, was the only other person who knew I was writing a book. If I had any doubt before, this made it all go away.

But the shifting was not just happening in my future as it related to work, but I also began to notice a shifting in my spirit. I started talking about God more to my husband and to my friends. It was no secret that I loved God and had faith in Him, but I rarely talked openly about Him, especially with my husband. He would often challenge me on some of my thoughts and rather than get into a discussion I would always shut down and end the conversation. Now I was starting those conversations and getting his thoughts.

I took a renewed interest in the Bible and began following one of those plans to read the Bible in a year. It wasn't that I wasn't already reading the Bible, but I always stuck to my favorite books which were all mostly in the New Testament in addition to Psalms and Proverbs. But now I craved more stories. I started breaking out my highlighter and pen as I made notes, highlighting scripture and calling my sister to say, "Girl, did you know?" A lot of the stories I knew or had read before but now I was seeing little nuggets that I missed before and it was exciting. I found the reading plan was too slow and I would just keep reading.

If you give it a chance, you'll find the stories in the Bible fascinating. They are better than any movie or television show you could ever watch. Not only has history continued to repeat itself over the years but God has remained the same. He truly is the same yesterday, today and forever more. And although sin and evil were just as rampant then as it is now, God always kept His promises, and He took care of His children. They thrived in a time when the world around them was becoming unbearable to contend with daily. He always made a way. He has not changed. And just as He took care of His children back then, He is taking care of us now. That should give us hope.

And so, as I began to shift, God's plan was starting to become more and more into focus. I still had no idea of how He planned to bring His plan to fruition but everyday my faith was strengthened. Every day I woke with expectancy as I began to watch and wait for His plan to unfold. I was now at the place where I truly believed that something new, was indeed happening in my life. I was beginning to see what my future held, and I was excited. All the promises and visions He promised and showed me since I was a little girl were starting to manifest. I knew I wasn't worthy, but my prayer was that I never failed Him. I wanted to be all He created me to be, and I never wanted to embarrass Him. I wanted my Father to be proud of me.

CONCLUSION

What Happens Now

> *For I know the plans I have for you, "declares the Lord", plans to prosper you and not to harm you, plans to give you hope and a future.*
>
> -Jeremiah 29:11

God desires the best for me. He desires the best for you. We miss that a lot of times because we are too busy looking at our current circumstances. He never said that our lives would be easy. He told us in Proverbs 3:5-6 to *Trust in the Lord with all your heart and lean not on your own understanding; in all your ways submit to Him, and He will make your paths straight.* In other words, you don't have to know where you are going or even how you'll get there. Don't try to reason why things are the way they are in your life. If you would just yield to Him, He'll make everything all right. He has big plans for you. Will you find yourself frustrated at times? Yes. Will you want to give in and throw in the towel? Absolutely. When it gets hard remember that He's always with you and He will never let you fall. You just have to trust Him.

I am so grateful for this new season in my life. I never knew I could find joy in tribulations yet here I stand. I am not sure where God is leading me, but I am more than happy to take the trip. I can't wait to tell you where I end up. Wherever it is, I pray it includes winning souls for Him. That would be a most amazing job.

When I first began the process of writing this book, I really wasn't sure where God was leading. I knew the main point would be sharing the importance of growing an intimate relationship with God, but I wasn't sure how I would be able to convince people that a relationship with God was worth their time. The only evidence I had was the evolution of my own relationship. I know my story is still incomplete and it may not be enough to make you pause to consider how great your life could be if you really gave Him a chance, but I ask that you at least consider it and reflect on the possibilities. I implore you to get out of the proverbial boat and focus on Jesus. And while you are mulling over your next move, think of doing a few other things:

1. Understand that while your denomination may give you a foundation in Christ, the essence of who He is can only be found in relationship with Him. He wants to be your personal savior. He wants to be your friend.

2. Understand that while it is important not to forsake the assembling of yourselves together, God still wants to meet with you and have one on one time with you. Carve out time for just the two of you daily. Talk to Him. Read His words. Meditate on Him. Listen to all the ways He speaks to you. You'll be amazed at what all He wants to share. He's a good listener and He gives the best advice! (He also knows how to keep your secrets!)

3. Recognize that He talks to you every day. He speaks to you through others. He speaks to you through His Word. And if you would just stop for a moment and shut out all the noise, you'll find He is speaking directly to you.

4. Never forget that He is yours and you are His. He promised never to leave or forsake you. He wants you to choose Him and He will never stop chasing you. Let Him catch you. I promise if you taste and see, you'll find that He really is good.

5. Allow Him to use you to reach others. If He tells you to deliver a message on His behalf, do it without hesitation. His sheep know His voice, so you'll know if it's Him. Only do what He asks, not what you propose in your own heart to do. Block out the noise of the world and listen to Him. He's always speaking.

6. Pray and pray all the time. He loves to hear from you. Yes, He knows all about what's going on in your life, but He loves that you think enough of Him to share your life with Him. He waits on you hoping you'll give Him some of your time. No one else can even begin to compare to Him.

7. If He tells you to get out of the boat, know that it's okay to do it afraid. He doesn't expect you to be all in, all the time, but He does want you to trust Him and know that He's not a man that He would lie. If He said it, He's going to do it. He's faithful.

8. Walk deeper into the river. Trust the river to take you on the most amazing adventures. You'll see and experience things your heart and mind never imagined.

9. Last, tell your story. Oh, the souls you will win for Him.

God loves you. Plain and simple. Remember "Neither height nor depth, nor anything else in all creation, will be able to separate us from the love of God that is in Christ Jesus our Lord. (Romans 8:39). There is literally nothing you can do to cause Him not to love you. He created you with purpose and it His desire that you fulfil that purpose. It is my sincerest prayer that God blesses you immensely. I pray that you get to experience His love in a way that has you longing for more of Him. Listen! Your destiny is calling. I need you to answer!

Printed in the United States
by Baker & Taylor Publisher Services